Straight Outta Ireland

TRUE STORIES OF IMMIGRATION, ADAPTATION, AND CELEBRATION

Edited by Edward McCann

650 | WHERE WRITERS READ

Founder / Editor • Edward McCann
Executive Producer • Richard Kollath
Literary Ombudsman / Senior Editor • Steven Lewis
Chief of Operations • Jane Kaupp
Design Director • Diane Fokas
Technical Advisor • Conrad Trautmann
Technical Advisor • Stephen Kaupp
Director of Photography • Kevin O'Connor
Videography/Photography • Sara Caldwell
Chief Audio Engineer • Jesse Chason
Copy Editor • Shelley Sadler Kenney

Advisory Committee

Rachel Aydt, Laura Shaine Cunningham,
Angela Davis-Gardner, Joseph Goodrich,
Jeremiah Horrigan, Arif Ilahi Khan, David Masello,
Honor Molloy, Irene O'Garden, John Pielmeier,
Susan Ragusa, James Russek, Angela Derecas Taylor,
Julie Trelstad, and Gretchen Reed

650 | Straight Outta Ireland

Sing your song. Dance your dance. Tell your tale.

— *Frank McCourt*

ABOUT 650

You'll find no shamrockery or paddywhackery in this volume; no overcooked corned beef and cabbage or warbled, teary renditions of "Danny Boy." What you'll find instead is a collection of rich personal stories reflecting the lived experiences of Irish and Irish-American writers—individual perspectives, skillfully presented with an emphasis on craftsmanship.

Originally performed for a live audience at New York's City Winery, the essays in this anthology were proudly presented as part of Carnegie Hall's citywide spring festival, "Migrations: The Making of America," acknowledging and honoring the perseverance and resilience of immigrants and the contributions they continue to make on America's diverse cultural landscape.

Read650 is a literary nonprofit with a mission to promote writers through live performances that celebrate the spoken word. It's a literary forum featuring two-page, 650-word personal stories that can be performed in five minutes. Our events at theaters, colleges, and libraries around the country are organized around single, broad topics that invite a range of expression, and recorded performances are added to a digital archive of writers reading their work aloud. The writers and their work receive additional exposure through podcasts, broadcasts, our YouTube channel, and in these printed volumes.

Read650 features graduate students and grandparents, first-timers and bestsellers. It's all about the writing; it's about the choice of one word over another, about the shape of sentences and paragraphs, the arc of a narrative, the poetry of a unique literary voice. If you love language and enjoy a good story, you've come to the right place. To submit your work or attend our shows, visit our website or Facebook page, and join our mailing list. Please tell your friends about us, and **spread the word about the spoken word.**

Ed McCann

Edward McCann, Founder / Editor

READ650.COM
FACEBOOK.COM/READ650

CONTENTS

Straight Outta Ireland

TRUE STORIES OF IMMIGRATION, ADAPTATION, AND CELEBRATION

Edited by Edward McCann

JULIA GAGLIARDI

Julia Gagliardi is a young writer at Fordham University studying English and sociology. A recipient of the 2016 Kate Herzog Writing Scholarship award and a finalist in the 2018 Stony Brook Short Fiction Prize, Julia's work has been published in Blue Marble Magazine, an online literary journal, and the *Comma*, Fordham University's literary magazine. Her website is www. julia-gagliardi.com.

THE FORTY FOOT

Julia Gagliardi

On the edge of Dún Laoghaire town, Brighid and I perch ourselves on the edge of the Forty Foot in swimsuits, white bathrobes, and brown boots and watch flocks of the elderly strip down to their knickers.

My mum's eldest sister cackles. "The perfect first sight in the morning. The bare arse of a feckin' old man."

The Forty Foot is a former gentlemen's only bathing place, carved out of the rock with changing stations open to both the air and the sea. The changing stations are painted a cerulean blue, but I never understood how the benches and walls were painted with the motley trinity of sideways rain, wind, and sea spray. The changing stations must have been dyed by the sea itself. On the benches, a crowd gathers in sagging bathing suits holding stout shot glasses, the color of crystalized ginger and brown bread, between thin fingers. One pours a clear liquor from an unmarked bottle. I know from the smell of sour barley that the bottle is *poitín*, moonlight liquor made in the bathtubs of Donegal. "Cheers," they say, raising their glasses.

Peering down with Bridghid and me onto the hushed celebrations of the swimmers is a Martello Tower, a squat, round

1

tower of gray stone. On top of the tower, a hundred years earlier in 1904, stood James Joyce. After he came forward up the winding stairs, mounted the round gun rest, and gazed over the bay of Sandycove, he composed the lines he'd write in the opening pages of Ulysses: "The sea, the snotgreen sea, the scrotumtightening sea."

Brighid disrobes and tugs one strap of her bathing suit over the pale, freckled curve of her shoulder. The chest of her navy-blue swimsuit is uneven. There is a hollow cove where her breast once was—breast cancer was an unwelcome visitor, but a mastectomy was a welcomed thief. When I was ten or eleven, I couldn't help but stare at the lopsided bathing suit, not because of her missing breast, but because I had never met a woman with a flat chest like mine.

I watch the swimmers changing into their suits as Brighid tucks blonde curls into a swimmer's cap. The older men are grumbling. Some of them have just returned from the sea with kelp jangling on their ankles. They take out clothes from a briefcase—pressed white shirts, dark pants, and brown loafers—and strip down from their used bathing suits. Others slowly undress from their tweed suits, unbutton their work shirts, and unlace their leather loafers. They carefully fold their underwear into tiny squares, slipped into the breast pocket of their coats.

We leave our belongings on the rocks and begin our descent towards the sea.

A staircase of rocks and a metal stairwell greased with kelp, drop into the water. Swimmers gingerly step down, a tightened grip on the metal bar of the stairwell. Sometimes bending down and splashing seawater on their arms, always shivering. The temperature of the water is below freezing.

Brighid dives into the water from the stairs, and swims back to the edge of the rocky outcrop, laughing, "You catch your moment of life and death here."

2

Once I start down these stairs, I cannot return upwards. No matter how long I climb, I never seem to get to closer to the bottom. The waves are kneading against the rocks. An older woman with a flowered swim cap stops me on my rocky descent.

"It's like bath water," she smiles. "Go on, but don't hesitate."

I dive headfirst into the sea. When my head breaks from the ceiling of the sea, my lungs are lost. I don't know whether the air should be coming in or out. I forget how to breathe. The sea is tricky. The longer I swim, the warmer the water is, but never truly warm.

Bridghid swims up next to me, laughing still, and cocks her head towards the older swimmers behind us. "If we can't outlast these feckers in the sea, we won't outlive them either. Go on, move your arms!"

We swim and swim, laughing, until we feel our limbs again

ANN FOLEY

Ann Foley was born in Dublin, Ireland and has lived in the New York City area for more than fifty years. She has degrees in nursing, psychology, and school psychology from the City University of New York and the College of New Rochelle and spent most of her career focusing on the needs of young children and young adults. Ann has three sons and three grandsons, she's an avid tennis player and an avid reader, and she has participated in a number of writing groups and workshops.

MARKING TIME

Ann Foley

I was seven years old in 1957 in Dublin where we lived on the top two floors above the family business, a pub. The only time the children were allowed in the pub was on Sunday when it was closed. Occasionally my mother took the five of us down to sit on the countertop with a bag of crisps and a mineral to watch TV while my father slept upstairs. Spending time together in the parlor upstairs was another special occasion usually at Christmas, with a lit fireplace.

With the smell of sweet brandy ignited on the Christmas pudding, all the good linen, bone china and silverware were laid out on the lemon-oiled mahogany table. My mother played seasonal tunes on the piano and my father added a wood log to the fire. As the youngest, I was so secure in my happiness that I wished it would never change. But after the Christmas crackers were pulled my mother confirmed the rumor that we would be moving to America. My brothers and sisters were excited, but I could tell by the audible change of breath that my mother was sad, and the official news alarmed me.

The plan was to move in stages. After my father left for New York, my mother and sisters went off to stay with relatives near the town of Ballinamuck, County Longford. One brother stayed in Dublin at boarding school and the other came with me to live for a while on Uncle Peter's farm in Drumlish, County Longford about seventy-five miles west of Dublin.

Separated from family, living on a farm, and going to a new school in the middle of the term, I felt afraid and disconnected, but I smiled and concealed my feelings. The evening before school I watched Aunt Kathleen cook over the open hearth and Uncle Peter light his pipe from a smoldering piece of turf plucked with tongs from the fire as he told us a story. My cousins were helpful, but they didn't tell me much about school. With a butterfly stomach I looked forward to it. That night I packed my schoolbag with a notebook, pencils, an eraser, a pen with extra nibs and inkbottle, lunch, a bottle of cocoa, and a piece of turf for the school fire.

On the way to school, my shoes pinched as I walked the long country road carrying my heavy leather brass-buckled schoolbag. In Dublin I went to school by bus and my schoolbag was as light as a scarf.

The nineteenth century schoolhouse had two classrooms each with a fireplace for heat and a single electric lightbulb dangling from each ceiling, added in the twentieth century.

After introducing me to the class, the teacher, Mrs. Lennon, invited all to place our bottles of tea or cocoa around the fireplace to heat up and instructed us to line up around the fire for warmth and to quiz us on sums. A school fireplace was mystifying to me.

Mrs. Lennon's face reddened and her eyes squinted after hearing several incorrect answers. As she took out her ruler, she yelled furiously, "Hold out your hands."

This is where I learned grit. In that moment, the teacher's fury resounding in my young ears, I caught a glimpse of how my father, raised on a poor farm, found the determination to start a new life in his teens in Dublin. I embraced the same sense of grit and waited patiently for a letter from America with instructions for my departure.

MAURA MULLIGAN

Maura Mulligan was born in County Mayo, Ireland where she worked on the family farm, learned to read in a two-room schoolhouse, and danced on the stage. She served pints in a bar at age sixteen and sailed to America at seventeen. In New York, she became a telephone operator and then a nun. After leaving the convent she returned to her roots and became an award-winning Irish step dancer and instructor, teaching Irish Céilí (folk) dance in Manhattan. Her writing has appeared in the *Irish Times*, the *Irish Echo*, *Irish America* magazine, and other publications. A speaker of Irish Gaelic and member of Irish American Writers & Artists, she is often interviewed on *Radio na Gaeltachta* (Irish language radio). Maura is the author of the memoir, *Call of the Lark*.

THE CROSSING

Maura Mulligan

When my Uncle Pake in New York wrote to ask if I wanted to fly or travel by ship. I said, "the ship would be best because it'll take longer. I don't want to leave Ireland in a hurry."

My plan was to ease my way over to New York, get a job, get rich, and pay my uncle back the passage money. Not yet seventeen, I was one of thousands leaving Ireland in the fifties.

The hackney driver drove slowly past our house when he saw Mam waving her white handkerchief from where she stood in front of our whitewashed, thatched cottage.

An eighteen-year-old neighbor, Teresa, also traveling alone, was at the train station. We'd make this journey together to America.

On the train to Cork, we wondered what our new lives would be like. I said I'd work for the telephone company and make calls to places like Tallahassee. We agreed we would not be maids.

At Cobh, people wept aloud, saying goodbye to daughters and sons. I cried too as the handkerchief wavers and the land on which they stood moved further away from the tender that ferried us toward the MV Britannic.

I envied the passengers traveling as a family unit. They would discover the unknown together. I was jealous of a sleeping child in her mother's arms. My mam was too sad to even come to the train station in Coillte Mach.

"Goodbye at home is hard enough *a grá*" she cried as she sprinkled me with holy water from Knock shrine.

Once on the ship, Teresa and I went in search of our sleeping quarters. Two English women were already settled in our four-bunk cabin. They'd boarded in Liverpool, the ship's port of departure. Our shipmates were not happy to see us.

"Blimey! Piss off, you young bogtrotters. This cabin's taken," the big blonde one lying on one of the lower bunks said. Her hair was in a French twist and the shade of her lipstick was a bright red. The other shipmate, less gaudy than the blonde, greeted our entrance with, "Bloody 'ell!." She stopped dabbing her eyelids with purple eye shadow, held the mirror in the air, and stared at her companion thoughtfully.

"Dunno, Liz. "There's four bleedin' bunks in 'ere."

Liz jumped up, angrily pushed her feet into a pair of garish-looking, gold-colored, sling-back high heels and left the cabin. When she returned, she was carrying a three-foot piece of rope—the likes of what you'd use to hobble a buck goat to stop him from wandering.

"Jesus, Mary & Joseph," I said as Liz proceeded to instruct us on how to be acceptable traveling companions.

"Now see 'ere. This side's ours, see—the English side. "Don't cross that bleedin' rope." She set the thick cord down in the middle of the narrow cabin floor, securing the line of division between Ireland and England. Her older companion, Jen said "blimey again. Then she advised Liz to "act civil."

The first night, I awoke to sounds of men's voices moaning from the English side. I lay frozen, worried that if the sailor lads got tired of Liz and Jen, they might try to move to our side. I had no high heel shoes to throw at them and make them go away.

Some nights while waiting on deck for the sailors to leave our cabin, Teresa and I would wonder about the future.

"Why are we going to America anyway?"

"I don't know, to get a job? Everyone is leaving home."

"I'll pay back the passage as soon as I get a job," I told Uncle Pake when he met me at New York Harbor.

"Greenhorns like you are in demand as maids," he responded.

"Not me," I said firmly. "I'll be a telephone operator and talk to people in strange places like Tallahassee."

IRENE O'GARDEN

Irene O'Garden has won or been nominated for prizes in nearly every writing category from stage to e-screen, hardcovers, as well as literary magazines and anthologies. Her critically-acclaimed play *Women on Fire*, played sold-out houses at Off-Broadway's Cherry Lane Theatre and was nominated for a Lucille Lortel Award. O'Garden won a Pushcart Prize for her lyric essay "Glad to Be Human," published by Untreed Reads. HarperCollins published Irene's first memoir, *Fat Girl*, and her new memoir, *Risking the Rapids: How My Wilderness Adventure Healed My Childhood*, was published by Mango in January 2019. Irene's poems and essays have been featured in dozens of literary journals and award-winning anthologies, and *Fulcrum*, published by Nirala, is the title of her first poetry collection.

SPIC AND SPAN

Irene O'Garden

When our trusty housekeeper retired, she recommended Rose. Meeting her, I had my doubts. Ours was a big house to pit against that petite frame, those narrow shoulders. But her smile beamed wide as a white picket fence. And there was that lovely pure Irish purr in her voice...

Her fine-boned body had born eight children, half still in grade school. Having grown up Irish Catholic with six siblings myself, I felt at once affectionate and concerned. Somebody's always sick. Tonsils flare. Collarbones snap. Measles spread like gossip in a small town. How could Rose ever work two consecutive weeks?

I hired her anyway. Sure enough, two weeks later something came up and Rose couldn't make it.

It would be the only time she cancelled in the next twenty spick and span years.

Rose was a month older than I, but when I was getting my freshman saddle shoes, she was emigrating to New York from a hearth-heated, lamplit cottage in the Irish countryside. She'd grown up with no electricity and no running water (unless you count how it ran from the skies in a ceaseless grey Irish drizzle.) She was a living link to the lives of my ancestors and a loving presence in ours.

She brought cleanliness and calm in a dedicated, cheery way, singing Christmas carols year-round as she worked.

"Will I polish the silver?"

"The windows need it. Will I do them?"

"They're callin' for frost this weekend. Will we bring the plants in?"

It was Rose we called if we got caught in the city and our parking was going to expire, or Kitty needed feeding, or the dog needed walking.

"No trouble at all, I'm just up the lane."

In the rare moments when she slowed, we talked of our families, of seasonal beauties, of the funny and the tragic in sweet, swift life.

And no matter what happened in her family or mine, she kept looking forward. "It's all good," she'd say.

Sure, there were places we didn't dwell. One bumper sticker on her green sedan read "I'm Catholic and I vote." Rose liked a little too much talk radio. A few too many cigarettes— her moment of Zen, puffing into the changing landscape. I worried about the bleach and cleaners she liked to use. She had diabetes and an iron disorder that necessitated monthly blood tests.

But mostly, it *was* all good. She instilled her own powerful work ethic in her children. Her strong young lads cleaned our basement, turned our couch toward the winter fireplace and toward the summer view, toted firewood, and set and stored the outdoor furniture.

Rose was determined, though, that no child of hers would ever clean house. She'd longed to be a nurse, an impossible fancy in her day, so she made certain all her eight graduated college. Education. Another Irish value.

She brought that nurse's tenderness turning down our bed, laying perfect, match-ready fires in the fireplace, so it was a sad day when she retired two Septembers ago.

"Thinkin' of movin' West near the children and grandchildren. Mike wants to move back to Ireland, but never," said Rose. "It's too much changed."

I took her to lunch, gave her a rose-shaped cross made of rose gold, and a poem I wrote commemorating her twenty years with us, never dreaming I would read it at her sudden funeral.

Rose flew out to visit her girls and consider the Westward move. On the homebound flight her great heart gave out. When they landed, she was rushed to a hospital while Mike waited at the airport, wondering why she hadn't deplaned. Her death was sudden, painless, with no suffering, they said. No hospital stay, no long goodbyes. Spic and span, just as Rose would have it.

COLIN BRODERICK

Colin Broderick, originally from County Tyrone, has lived in New York for the past thirty years. His is the author of two memoirs, *Orangutan* and *That's That*, and he's the editor of the just-published essay collection, *The Writing Irish of New York*. Colin is also a film maker who has written and directed two feature movies, *Emerald City* and *"That's That*. His website is www.colinbroderick.com

AN IRISH WRITER IN NEW YORK

Colin Broderick

The New York I arrived in twenty-eight years ago was one of abandoned buildings, battered window shades, and blackened shells along the highway. Uptown were boom-box, squeegee men, and sneaker wars. Down on The Deuce they were shilling sleaze and switchblades for as cheap as a buck. Pickpockets, peddlers, and preachers stood shoulder to shoulder with ruddy-faced Irish American cops too outnumbered and sweaty to give a goddamn. Back then, forty-second street was a scabbed vein, so pock marked and contaminated it was practically its own ecosystem.

Downtown was squatters-rights, artists, and dope dealers, alongside old-school Eastern- European grandmothers in headscarves lugging shopping bags up Second Avenue. Street walkers bold as peacocks preened themselves on the cobbled-stoned streets of the West Village while over around Saint Mark's, pale faced boys in skinny pants and Mohawks graffitied shuttered tenement walls and nodded out in Tompkins Square Park. New York was a city of shadows and ghosts and blocks you didn't dare venture down alone.

It was a town that felt lived in. A town with an active working class. Madness and danger were a staple of everyday life.

Not that it was easy; it was a hustle. It was a dodge and a weave, blindfolded and drunk through a minefield. Each new step possibly your last. But man was it alive; an urban landscape so rich in story that words practically rained down off the fire escapes like rust chips and danced their way into my soul in ready-made paragraphs.

Being young and Irish in New York I was bequeathed the added romance of a literary heritage, even if I didn't understand it fully back then.

New York is where Irish literature comes to get its passport stamped.

As a young writer I had a dream that one day I would see my name on the spine of a book, on a shelf, wedged next to Banville and Behan.

There was only one small catch: I couldn't write.

I could drink though. Boy could I drink!

So I drank … I worked construction, fell in and out of love … and marriages, like a man possessed.

In the summer of 2006 I was 38 years old, living in a fifth-floor walk-up in Hell's Kitchen. I weighed 115 pounds. I was unemployable. I was somehow surviving on a diet of beer, vodka, weed, and cocaine. In my alcoholic madness I had been stabbed, beaten, jailed and hospitalized. The idea of taking a swan dive off my fifth-floor balcony onto ninth avenue had begun to haunt me as a viable alternative to the chorus of demons that plagued my every waking thought.

One night laying in the dark alone, sipping on whiskey, listening to the blare of traffic below my window, I finally understood that this was the place right before death. If something didn't change soon they would find me here on the floor of this apartment surrounded by empty bottles. This was the end. It had to be. I moved to a friend's farmhouse upstate and began to write like my life depended upon it. It did.

Within a year I'd sold my drinking memoir, *Orangutan*, to Random House.

Over the last eleven years without a drink I published three books, directed two of my own plays, saw my name in *The New Yorker* and the *New York Times,* and took the stage at Lincoln Center to read my own work. I wrote and directed two feature movies. I met my wife, and I became a father to a girl and then a boy. I am not rich. I am not a household-name author. But I am still writing. In my own roundabout way, I wound up living the very life that I'd always dreamed might be possible. I am an Irish writer in New York.

JOHN GREDLER

John Gredler has been published in *Narratively, Atticus Review, The Sun magazine, Westchester Review* and other publications. John was awarded the 2014 Kathryn Gurfein Writing Fellowship from The Writing Institute at Sarah Lawrence College and is a regular contributor to Read650. John lives with his family in Tuckahoe, New York.

BILLY MULLIGAN

John Gredler

Most of the tenants had Irish surnames. Callahan sat all day at his window facing Third Street, selling cigarettes for a quarter each. Quigley worked as a waiter at the Second Avenue Deli, his white jacket and black pants a size too small for his tall, lanky body. After work every day he sat in his room drinking a six of Rheingold pint cans. Bobby Healy spent his days at the OTB parlor betting the horses; his poison was Richard's Wild Irish Rose, the flat pint empties covering his floor.

The SRO hotel—SRO for single room occupancy— was on East Third Street just off the Bowery, originally two identical brick three-story row houses that had been converted in the 1940s. The façade still showed ghostly outlines of the two stoops replaced now by a single street level doorway that opened into a central staircase. On each of the three levels was a hallway lined with single rooms, nine to a floor with a shared bathroom at the end.

The rooms were eleven feet long by six feet wide with high ceilings and a tall window. Each had a white enameled cast iron sink attached to the wall, with a medicine cabinet above. Most rooms still had the original furniture— a metal frame bed with a single mattress on springs, a wooden two-door wardrobe, a bedside table and maybe a bentwood chair. A bare bulb on the ceiling with a chain hanging down. Some rooms also had a hot plate, and a few had a small refrigerator.

The shades on the windows looked like ancient yellowed parchment from the years exposed to cigarette smoke. The walls of some of the rooms were so thick with nicotine they looked varnished. Some of the men who lived there also had a sallow hue as if the years spent smoking and drinking in those small spaces had left them like cured meat.

The rich, acrid odor of decades of captured smoke mixed with beer, wine, rotgut booze, body odor, urine, and bay rum cologne was concentrated in these chambers.

Billy Mulligan worked across the Bowery as a desk clerk at the White House, the last of the big SRO hotels that used to line the avenue. He was short, pear- shaped with an oval balding head, and a large nose crazed with burst capillaries. He wore wirerimmed glasses over his watery blue eyes and was always dressed in a suit. The cuffs of his shirts were frayed and the sleeves of his jacket shiny at the elbows.

Mulligan spoke with a deep raspy voice that he claimed was caused by mustard gas that he inhaled during "The War." All these guys had stories; the one they told you usually wasn't the real one.

Billy went to mass at Grace Church every Sunday. There was a dust- encrusted plastic crucifix with a rosary wrapped around it above his bed. Faded pictures of Cardinal Spellman and Pope John XXIII hung on his wall.

One day he came down to tell me he was moving. When he brought the few things he owned downstairs he apologized to me for leaving his room a mess. He pulled me aside, holding my arm and talking in a low voice as he looked up at me. "John, I couldn't take everything. Please just throw it all out, I'm sorry." He pressed some bills into my hand as he said goodbye.

His room was cleaner than most. Under the bed was a cheap suitcase. When I opened it, I saw it was full of pornographic pulp novels, some of them pretty raunchy. Almost all of them were gay themed. A lot of S&M and bondage.

I saw that the picture of Cardinal Spellman had fallen to the floor behind the bed, the glass cracked. I picked it up, put it in the suitcase on top of the books and dragged it all out to the trash can on the corner.

ANTHONY MURPHY

Anthony C. Murphy is originally from Lancashire, England and has worked on the spoken word scene in the UK and New York City, both as a performer and an assistant producer. He's the author of the novel, *Shiftless*, a fictional romp about growing up in the north of England. He's also written an illustrated children's book, *Liberty Takes a Break*, which isn't as bleak as it sounds. He lives in Yonkers, New York.

ANOTHER FAMILY PLOT

Anthony Murphy

"So?" The barmaid asks.

"A pint of that," I point but she questions my attitude.

"What's up?"

"I lost my dad," I sigh.

"Uh huh!" She's listening. "Have you phoned anyone?"

"It's not like that. He was in an urn," I say. "My bag was stolen. I was at a party."

"Well. Okay… Where did you last see him?" She asks, matter-of-factly.

"Dublin," I say. And she laughs. She snorts a big one and curses and crosses herself to keep the demons at bay. "Holy Feckin' Jeezus! Do you even know where ye are?"

"No." I say.

"Well, I hope you said your goodbyes!" She says and tuts at me.

"Yeah." I say. "Not really. I just brought the ashes from England to get buried back in Cork."

"Here." She says, handing me a pint. "You're in Wicklow!" She shakes her head.

"Thanks!" I do remember the train, vaguely.

The beer burns my throat, but I don't care. I wonder if this has happened before. The stealing of an urn! It must have happened before. Maybe they thought there was something valuable in it?

I sit there sipping and feeling sorry for myself. A few more patrons enter the pub and are familiar with me. The barmaid lights a fag and blows the smoke out of the side of her mouth and picks a piece of tobacco out of her teeth, I guess, it could be something else. "So, what are you going to do?"

"Can I get one of those?" I ask, pointing to her cigarette.

"No." She considers. "You have to earn it."

I am feeling hungry now with my emptied belly. I look about the bar but they don't have much. "Can I get a pickled egg please?"

"Sure. It's your funeral.... Sorry!"

"I like them." I say. I tuck into it, it's like a chemistry lesson exploding in my mouth, but it helps with my reality, it gives me a jolt. "Can I collect glasses for you tonight?" I ask, cheeks full of acidic protein, "Then I can earn it."

She thinks. "Why not?" She puffs. "But I tell you, it's quiet on Mondays." She gives me one of her cigarettes. I agree with her but I have a lot going on. I have to get to across the country for the funeral service and I have no remains to bury. Where are you? My head is clear as a hangover. I check my socks for the little cash I have left.

"Can I have the whole jar of eggs please? And another pint."

"Where are you going with this?" She asks, but she gives me the jar. The weight and size of it are comparable to the urn. Of course it's glass and not plastic, I'll have to explain something to my Aunt Maureen, but not that I haven't got my dad with me.... And there are only ten eggs left. "It's doable!" I say to no one in particular.

"Sure. Weirdo!" she says.

"Okay, everyone, the pickled eggs are on me! Do it for the old feller!" I shout and raise the jar aloft with both hands like I've just won the cup. I hear one whoop and I have a few takers, although I have to eat most of the eggs myself. It's a chastening experience. I know I can throw them away but that's such a waste! I probably won't eat for a while anyway. My stomach revolts a little but I manage.

All night I collect empties for my new friends and clean out the ashtrays, I stash all of their fag ash in the old pickle jar. Later, I have to sift it a little, to separate the butts, yet at least I have a new dad, although he's lost weight and he smells of vinegar and old smoke... but sure he would anyway. I tighten the lid on him.

CHARLES R. HALE

Charles R. Hale was born, raised, and educated in New York City, a descendant of Irish famine immigrants. His historically themed essays have appeared in literary magazines and in the book, *The Writing Irish of New York*. A chronicler of New York life and culture, Charles produces shows blending New York's rich history with music and art. His shows, including *A Musical History of the Lower East Side, New York City: A Shining Mosaic, Jazz in the City*, and *Crossing Boroughs* have been performed throughout the metropolitan area. Charles is a co-founder of Artists Without Walls, an organization created to inspire, uplift, and unite people and communities of diverse cultures through the pursuit of artistic achievement. charlesrhaleproductions.com

WE ARE AS ONE

Charles R. Hale

I tell stories. How could I do otherwise...my father and grandfather were inveterate storytellers. "We Irish love a good story." "We're Irish... and proud to be." Yet, curiously, no one ever spoke of Ireland.

My connection to Ireland? I confessed to Irish priests—Reilly, Reagan, and McCarthy—and St. Patrick's Day, a one-day, unholy mess of Irish excess. Truth be told, I grew up Catholic, not Irish. Sunday Mass and Catholic Youth Organization dances, Catholic schools and confraternity. The stations of the cross and confession served as constant reminders, as if we could forget, that we were Catholic first...any and all nationalities second.

My family names, however, rang of Ireland—Kelly, Sullivan, Horrigan and Lyons. Fourteen of my sixteen great-great grandparents emigrated from Ireland to New York City. But as each new wave of ancestors surged ashore, each successive generation washed over the rest, leaving few traces of familial or cultural inheritance. Perhaps it was better to forget. When my ancestors died, their voices and stories vanished with them. All but one.

"My father was working in the family butcher shop in Castleblayney when the trouble started," my maternal grandfather, Allie, said of his father, George Gorman. "A policeman entered the shop and started cuffin' him around. My father was only fifteen, but he didn't take guff from anyone. I'm afraid he responded…and then some. That night, in the winter of 1888, my father packed a bag and left for America. He never saw his family or Ireland again." That was the only story that linked me to my Irish ancestry.

Twenty years ago, my family and I, including my mother, Dorothy Gorman Hale, visited Castleblayney where we had arranged to meet a local who grew up near the family farm. We drove a mile from town, turned onto a dirt road, and soon the old rundown farmhouse, which was used for storage by the current owner, appeared. My mother entered the house while my family and I walked the property. Soon we too entered the house where my mother was silently standing in front of the fireplace, staring. And although she didn't express it as such, my mother appeared to be on a pilgrimage and was, at last, standing in front of a holy shrine. I waited, not knowing what she was feeling. I felt my mother's emotions gather.

"It's the first time I've ever felt my father was connected to something," she said. "All we knew was when he was a child he lived a miserable existence on the streets of New York City, but it was as if nothing or no one came before his childhood. It's the first time I've ever felt warmth for my grandfather George. No one ever had anything nice to say about him, but now, that seems so insignificant as does his reason for coming to America. But standing here, in the house where my grandfather was born, I just feel better knowing there really is a link, a connection between my father, my grandfather, and Ireland."

My family didn't speak about the past yet the roots of my existence are intertwined and braided in the stories of men and women like George Gorman, my mother, and those who have gone before them. I often think of my mother standing in front of the fireplace, the expressiveness of her silence more powerful than any words.

It was in my mother's moment of silence that I recognized how we are as one, truly, of each other, and how stories connect the past to the present.

Stories connect us.

I tell stories so I never forget.

CARI PATTISON

Cari Pattison is an ordained Presbyterian minister who spent twelve years doing pastoral work at The Reformed Church of Bronxville in Westchester County, New York. She also teaches barre classes and trained as a Jazzercise, yoga, and Pilates instructor. She's originally from Kansas City and has a background in teaching.

Cari has blogged for The Huffington Post, illustrated the children's book *ABC: Sing With Me*, and is a 2015 recipient of the Kathryn Gurfein Fellowship at The Writing Institute at Sarah Lawrence College. She's written for the faith phone app d365.org and contributed a chapter to Shannon Smythe's *Women in Ministry: Questions and Answers in the Exploration of a Calling*.

SOMEONE TO WATCH OVER ME

Cari Pattison

"What are you doing? Don't get into that car!" my dad yells, charging up the sidewalk of Limerick. He appears to have gotten his front tooth knocked out.

I step out of the small gray Peugeot.

There is something so dear about being thirty-five and newly single and your dad trying to save you from kidnappers in Ireland.

Does it count as kidnapping if you're old enough to be president of the United States? Older than Jesus when he got crucified? I am leaving a Bible study that I found while on vacation with my parents. Going to Ireland together is what you do right after you get divorced and your dad is into genealogy.

Upon arrival in Limerick, we discover that most of the shops near our hotel were boarded up and it was the first time I'd seen so many young people who looked like me, appearing to be homeless. It has rained every day we've been here, holding steady at windy and cloudy and forty-nine degrees Fahrenheit. In *July*. I needed something other than the weather to lift my spirits. On Sunday we attended some kind of storefront church that suited my dad's request for "as close to Presbyterian as possible."

The service left me cold, so I went into spiritual-tourist mode, which led me to said Bible study. I have a way of sniffing out the most underground prayer meetings and upstart church plants. For me, going to worship wherever I want is a precious jewel I had to give up when I became a minister.

And speaking of precious jewels, I'd recently returned my engagement ring to my ex. Maybe I could find a Claddagh ring here with tourmaline, a stone said to promote inspiration, reduce fear, and build confidence: bridging the physical with the spiritual.

In this moment I stood on the cobbled road of a woebegone Irish town, desperate to bridge *something*, anything: the world of wife to ex-wife, house to apartment, minister to disillusioned doubter, little girl to grown-up.

When my parents used to go on weekly date nights, I'd stay awake till I heard the garage door, praying they'd arrive home safe — neither drinking too much nor getting in an accident. I don't recall ever seeing them drunk, nor did they ever not return safe. But from first through sixth grade, I knew my prayers were the secret to their welfare. Always it was me trying to protect them.

But now, twenty-five years later, my dad stands by this Irish Peugeot, the paternal look in his eyes so fierce I fear he might punch the man opening the door. He should know by now that his daughter saves all her risky behavior for God. Or what feels like God's leading, anyway. Two years in Kenya. Teaching in the inner city. Taking leave of a bad marriage.

"Dad!" I want to say, "don't worry. These people are from the Irish Brethren Church and I found out about their Bible study from a window flyer. They barely have two cents to their name, but they take Jesus' words so to heart that when he says, 'lend to anyone who asks of you,' they give all their tools away, even though their neighbor never gives them back. They prayed for me, Dad, and offered me a ride back to the hotel 'cause it's getting dark and it's downtown Limerick, and *it's all okay!*"

But I don't say a thing.

I bask in the forgotten glow of my father's love, a love ready to come to blows to rescue me from Bible-toting Irish assailants.

The group leader turns to me, concerned. "Do you know this man?"

As my dad gets closer, I see that his missing tooth is nothing more than a piece of food covering up his incisor – a black olive, by the looks of it.

"Yes," I laugh. "I think I do."

DREW MINTER

Drew Minter is an internationally known countertenor who, for over three decades, sang leading roles in the opera houses of Brussels, Toulouse, Boston, Washington, Santa Fe, and other around the world. He has sung with many of the world's foremost baroque orchestras and made over seventy recordings. A featured guest at festivals such as Ravinia, The Brooklyn Academy of Music's Next Wave, Tanglewood, Marlboro, Boston Early Music, and Edinburgh, Drew is also an active opera stage director who directed regularly for the Goettingen International Handel Festival, Boston Midsummer Opera, and Boston's Opera Aperta, among others. Drew has written over a hundred reviews and critical pieces for *Opera News* and *Oxford University Press Journal* and is a senior lecturer at Vassar College where he's taught music for two decades.

DEAD SLOW

Drew Minter

The first evening in Dublin, our friend Fiona drove us up into some high hills above Rathsfarnum for a few pints at a pub our Irish friends called "trad, but not boring." I noticed that Fiona was taking things at a good clip on perilously narrow roads but having grown up with a back-seat driving mother, I kept my cautionary comments to myself. Nonetheless, I was unprepared when our forced proximity on a stretch of road led us to connect with an oncoming car, clipping each other's side-view mirrors. Without losing a beat, Fiona and the other driver were out on the street. I expected heated, raised voices; instead, flashing abashed smiles, they exchanged cards, and within two minutes we were headed on to the pub, mirror dangling while the other driver, sporting a similarly hanging appendage, rushed on to his destination. Irish affability is notorious, but this was ridiculous.

This incident was my introduction to the art of driving in the Emerald Isle. Some days later my husband and I collected our rental, a sleek grey Renault wagon. I set my mind to do some serious cruising around Kilkenny, while James was taking part in a harp conference for the week. Foregoing even a spin around the parking lot, I pressed the clutch with my right foot, giving it gas with my left while using my left hand to change gears. Everything was opposite, but miraculously, it all hooked up! My hat size nearly doubled with my early driving success. I felt like an accomplished hand at a new pinball game. Every reversed roundabout became a new 500-point score.

While James improved his string technique, I improved my game, driving out to newer and more remote locations to paint: deserted abbeys, sheep meadows, rocky peat fields, wells blessed by Celtic saints. Driving toward Cappoquin one day, I followed the Blackwater River. I stopped to paint the picturesque ruins of Kells Priory, stepping lively over the fields of cow patties and sheep dip in search of better perspectives. Much put-out bovines cast their jaundiced eyes upon my watercolors. Evenings found me in a Kilkenny pub: downing glasses of Guinness, glorying in the day's kelly green vistas, proud of my explorations.

But my joy came in the driving itself. Irish country roads have a way of curving deliciously as they narrow to a point where only one car can pass at a time. Usually, you find a little "lay by," the quaint English term the Irish use to denote where it's wisest to hang back. Example: when a large caravan or tourist bus is bearing down on you. Vehicular size is everything in Ireland.

En route to Kildare, the hedgerows looming on either side, I found myself on just such a serpentine stretch one morning. Before me, painted on the country road pavement in bright yellow caps: "SLOW." Little bothered, I rounded a bend and was greeted by the words "VERY SLOW". Now this gave me pause. A new kind of marking and following so soon upon the other. Another bend yielded the legend "DEAD SLOW." I slowed. Sure enough, coming toward me was a sizable lorry but no lay-by to be seen and the opaque hedgerows now at least ten feet in height.

"He who hesitates is lost," was one of my one one-eighth Irish mother's favorite slogans, whether applied to driving or general service. With reliable wrong-side-of-the-road dexterity, flexing my pinball flippers, I gunned it and shifted, pulling in the nick of time past a Mercedes truck. Had I known it was a Mercedes, I might have yielded. The truck was forced to drop a gear. Passing by, I awaited an angry gesture, maybe the finger. Instead, the lorry driver smiled, saluting me with that same customary Irish affability. My score? 1000 points and an extra game.

HONOR FINNEGAN

Honor Finnegan has been singing and performing since she was a child. She was in the first national tour of *Annie*, she performed at the ImprovOlympic, Chicago's premiere venue for improvisational comedy, and she has won accolades for songwriting and performing folk music. After a dramatic experience in 2016 involving a flash flood in Texas, Honor began writing first person essays and participating in slams at The Moth. She is also a preschool educator/special educator, a Heartfulness meditation trainer, and mother to one adult son. She currently resides in Dubai, where she teaches Pre-K at the Bank Street-affiliated Clarion School.

BUTTERMILK LANE

Honor Finnegan

My husband and I were musicians living on the west coast of Ireland, which meant we were living on the dole. The dole, if you don't know, is welfare, but it pays better, and there's less humiliation. We topped it up with gig money, and we did okay that way. It was grand, as they say. My favorite way to earn a few extra bob was busking in the superlative acoustics of Buttermilk Lane.

Buttermilk Lane is a thin walkway between Middle Street and St. Nicholas Collegiate Church in Galway City. I could go out at my leisure, sing acapella, and wait for the sound of an Irish pound coin dropping in my case. This was before the Euro. The Irish punt was a beautiful thing. Wider and thinner than a silver dollar, it was elegant, with an elk on one side and a Celtic harp on the other. Poetry to look at, music to my ears when it hit the vinyl vanity that I used for collecting coinage. Occasionally, I got hassle from a shopkeeper or traveler, but mostly I met sweet old women coming from church after the mass or saying of the rosary. "Lovely singing", they'd say. "What part are you from?," meaning what part of Ireland. They thought I was Irish. There was no higher compliment.

Irish American = Irish wannabe. It's a fact. Even some non-Irish have a thing for Ireland. Celtophiles, I suppose. I'm no longer one, but in my twenties, I felt an unspeakable pull to the island of my mother's, mother's, mother's mother. Not long after arriving in Ireland, I became a mother myself.

When my son was about a month old, I was out of my mind with breastfeeding and being holed up indoors. I put the baby in the pram and headed up to Buttermilk Lane. It had been a while since I'd gone busking, and I'd never been busking with a baby before, but I didn't have a childminder, so I parked the pram, got out my case, and started in on a verse of "She Moves Through the Fair". The old women love that one.

Oh, the acoustics in Buttermilk Lane! It's like butter, but better. It's like a church without a ceiling. The thin, Medieval path opens skyward toward the heavens, usually overcast with clouds, but still—you can't get closer to heaven than the heavens.

I'd been singing for about fifteen minutes when a famous Irish musician stopped to listen. He turned his back to me, posturing his body in faux inconspicuous Irish fashion, and when I was done, he came over and introduced himself. I knew who he was. He said the band was reforming and looking for a new singer. Now, this was no pub band. This band played music festivals and concert halls all over the world. It was a real opportunity, one I had half-jokingly said I would get some day. I was very excited. We arranged to talk and meet the following afternoon.

We met, played some tunes, and after some deliberation, I was in. I could join the ranks of Dolores Keane, Mary Black, and Maura O'Connell but something didn't set right. I couldn't help noticing the band wasn't the happiest of campers, and more importantly, they didn't want me to take my baby on tour.

I thought about it. World travel, good money, a springboard to a solid career as a singer. Dirty diapers, endless suckling, and no sleep.

Hmmm... I kind of kicked myself later, but you know what I did.

I figured, if I got desperate for singing, I could go to Buttermilk Lane, put my case down... "Twas down by the glenside, I met an old woman..." and they would come out of the church and say, "I heard you inside. It sounded like an angel singing."

Plus, there was always the dole.

JACK O'CONNELL

Jack O'Connell is a New York City native presently living on Long Island with his wife, Margaret. He is a working actor with extensive stage and film credits including *Doubt, Big Night, Inside Llewyn Davis, The Paper, God's Pocket, The Quitter, Brazzaville Teenager, Everyday People, The Yards,* and others. His numerous TV credits include *Mad Men, Nurse Jackie,* and *Vinyl,* and Jack is currently seen in a recurring role on the Netflix hit *The Marvelous Mrs. Maisel,* playing Jerry, the elevator operator. Jack is a member of Artists Without Walls.

THE END OF THE PARADE

Jack O'Connell

On March 16, 1976 my friend Brian O'Neill and I each rented white tie and tails from Nat's Evening Wear on Francis Lewis Boulevard in Queens. We showed up on 44th Street in Manhattan at ten-thirty the next morning to march in the 215th annual St. Patrick's Day Parade.

With springs of clover on our lapels, we were complete imposters. Two "narrow backs" who called in sick to their day jobs, Brian as a case worker for The Department of Social Services, me a case unloader on a Pepsi truck. Terrance Cardinal Cooke was giving his blessing as we stepped off about one hundred yards behind the grand marshall, Governor Hugh Carey. Seventeen blocks uptown, in front of the Pierre Hotel, we drank a toast to the day.

"Who are you guys?" The doorman asked with a laugh. "Lord Urine of Surrey" O'Neill answered in a perfect British accent, adding "and I'm in a hurry."

We were waving to crowds lined up behind police barriers, enjoying every minute of the parade and our charade. As we made the column right onto 86th Street, the chatter became louder as

45

cops and firefighters fell out of ranks. Many were already holding cups that magically appeared. As we crossed Lexington and then Third Avenue the Yorkville street cafes were lined up like chairs. The Bremen Hause, The Lorelei, Heidelberg, The Bavarian Inn and others—German Beer Halls now filling up with this city's cross section of nationalities and religions. I heard Judy Garland belting it out from some juke box, "It's a great day for the Irish, it's a great day for fair." Cops and firemen sang along in their Paddy's Day brogues with the Clancy Brothers' "The Wild Colonial Boy." St. Vincent's Hospital nursing students in navy blue capes were pretending to jig with white stockinged legs kicking up a storm. Pipers sitting now, holding hats in their laps after the two-and-a-half-mile march. Orange, green and white sashes that read Mayo, Sligo and Meath among others.

Brian and I eventually found ourselves seated at a long wooden table with a group of alumni from Providence College. They were here for a basketball tournament their school was participating in. The National Invitation Tournaments in those days always seemed to fall during the week of the parade. This group had rented an entire floor of rooms plus a party suite at The Taft Hotel on Seventh Avenue. After a while we all went off in a fleet of yellow taxis to continue on with the party.

We drank more beer and sang song after song until exhausted. I stretched out on the floor of a wall closet, removed my shoes, rolled my jacket up for a pillow, loosened my tie, and slept.

Next, I recall an Irish hotel security man pulling me by my ankles from the wall closet. "These Irish are the most charming, imaginative, worthless people we produce" he said to the waiting staff. Then he turned to me: "Be gone with you so the maids can work. And your mate, The Urine Lord, is looking for ya."

On my train I opened a newspaper and read the headline. FOUR DEAD WHEN CAR BOMB EXPLODES! The story began, "Four people, thought to be part of a Catholic bar crowd celebrating St. Patrick's, were killed on March 17th. The Hillcrest Bar in Dungannon, County Tyrone was the target for religious reasons.

I stepped into the cubbyhole train lavatory and became sick. As I looked at my reflection in the stainless-steel towel dispenser, I saw a jerk in a wrinkled, rented tuxedo singing "It's a Great Day for the Irish" when it was suddenly not that way at all.

EDWARD McCANN

Edward McCann is an award-winning writer/producer and the founder and editor of Read650, a literary forum that celebrates the spoken word with live events in New York City and elsewhere. A frequent contributor to *Milieu* magazine, Ed's features and essays have been published in many literary journals, anthologies, and national magazines, including the *Sun, Country Living, the Irish Echo, Better Homes & Gardens, Good Housekeeping* and others. His essay, "Pregnant Again," was selected for the anthology, *Listen To Your Mother*, published by Putnam. He lives and writes in the Hudson River Valley.

IRISH SODA BREAD

Edward McCann

With another St. Patrick's Day approaching, I've assembled the tools and ingredients to make my late mother Mildred's Irish soda bread. I pre-heat the oven to 375 degrees, slip an apron over my head and tie it around my waist, and then measure flour, salt, and baking soda into a glass bowl. Reaching for the sugar and butter, I consider the countless loaves of bread Mom baked during her ninety-four years. I only make this bread in March, and for me its pleasures—both the making and the sharing—are linked not only with my memories of Mom, but also with the last days of winter, the promise of spring, with its brighter days and budding trees, and a yearning to return once again to my ancestral home in Ireland's Golden Vale; to Mitchelstown, Kilmallock, and Tipperary.

The St. Patrick's Day card that arrived yesterday from my sister, Betty, is the only card I'm likely to receive this year and prompted memories of the green envelopes of every shade that once filled in the glossy, black mailbox of my childhood home in Broad Channel, Queens. Those greeting cards arrived from aunt Ceal and from cousins Ethel and Edna and Geraldine and Dottie; from aunt

49

Millie and uncle Harold and other family we rarely saw throughout the year—and who are now mostly all gone. Mom displayed these cards on our polished Magnavox television set, an eye-level tableau of leprechauns and rainbows and shamrocks; of St. Patrick and the snakes; of ruddy-looking men in caps; of freckle-faced, red haired children; of winding paths leading to forlorn, thatched cottages; of gray horses in emerald fields; and of pints of Guinness and pots of gold.

Those images—paired with television scenes of the parade and the sounds of The Chieftains and The Clancy Brothers on the turntable—shaped an abiding sense of my heritage. On St. Patrick's Day morning, I'd awaken to a delicious aroma and then descend to the kitchen to find Mom kneading lumps of dough while fresh loaves of soda bread cooled nearby. Few things transport me to childhood like a slice of that warm bread, a pat of butter melting and pooling amid raisins and caraway seeds. It's my Queens-born, Irish-American equivalent of Proust's madeleine.

Soon I'm thinking of my Irish grandfather, Jack, who, the story goes, emigrated with his family to Brooklyn at the age of three. Though he never returned to Ireland, he retained the faint brogue of his parents and older siblings. "I can say something you children can't," Grandpa liked to joke, adding, "I came into this country with me pants on!"

I smile to myself and add raisins and caraway seeds to the mixture before me, then stir in the buttermilk. With flour coating my hands, I turn the cool lump of dough onto the board and knead it lightly, shaping it into a round loaf. Then I transfer the loaf to a buttered, cast-iron skillet, slash the top with a deep "X", and slide it into the oven.

Grandpa Jack, who disdained the fake, once-a-year, just-add-water Irishness that seems to demand overcooked corned beef and cabbage and "Danny Boy," would never know that his daughter and grandchildren would return not only to the old sod, but to the townland and road and actual home of his birth. He'd never know about the loving friendships we'd develop with our Irish cousins who welcomed us "home," and of the long visits we now share both in Ireland and America, the ocean no longer a barrier between us. And he'd never know that I, only one generation removed, would one day reclaim my Irish citizenship.

When my fresh loaf of bread has cooled enough to handle, I break through its browned crust with a serrated knife to cut and butter a slice, and then sit down with a cup of hot tea. I glance at my watch, calculate the time in Ireland, and reach for the phone.

MALACHY McCOURT

Malachy McCourt was born in Brooklyn but raised from age three in Limerick, Ireland. Returning to New York at twenty, he worked manual jobs until becoming an actor, a career including roles on Broadway, off-Broadway, on television, and in film. He's been published in *New York Newsday, National Geographic, the New York Times* and elsewhere. With brother, Frank, he co-authored the play *A Couple of Blaguards* and has written his own New York Times bestselling memoir, *A Monk Swimming*. Other books include a second memoir, *Singing My Him Song, Danny Boy, The Claddagh Ring, Voices of Ireland*, an anthology, and *Malachy McCourt's History of Ireland*. Happily married to Diana for more than four decades, his most recent book is entitled, *Death Need Not Be Fatal*.

MY AMERICAN DREAM

Malachy McCourt

Some of us not raised in the USA romanticize the life of Americans. We imagine tree-lined avenues with motorcars parked in driveways; we imagine cheery families with beautiful white teeth and warm dispositions living in lovely homes with lawns and flowerbeds, all lit by a friendly sun.

When you grow up abroad you dream of this American life, not imagining that there is poverty here, too, along with disease and disability; you don't think about the laborers, garbage removers, street sweepers, gas station attendants, maids, and gardeners; you don't think about crime and criminals, the jailed and the jailers, or of a populace dreaming of a better life—perhaps elsewhere than America.

I did not dream of going to America to do anything for America, I just thought and dreamt of what it would do for me. I knew I wanted to avoid manual labor and not to have to work outdoors. And while I couldn't know just what I would do once I got there, I daydreamed a vision of myself entering a huge office building where I took a lift to ascend to a very high floor. There, a series of desk-bound secretaries would greet me with "Good morning, Mr. McCourt," as I made my way to an office where I'd spend my days making important decisions.

It did not quite turn out that way.

I got a menial job washing dishes, and I did manual labor on the docks. I did some other work loading trucks and bartending before I began acting and appearing on radio and TV shows. As my life in America became more interesting and complicated, I married, fathered two children, and divorced. I remarried, became a father again, ran for governor, wrote books and a play with my brother, Frank, and I now have eight grandchildren with a great grandchild on the way. It's been a rich and interesting life, and while I owe much to America, I participated in doing something important for America, too.

My beloved wife, Diana, had a child with a developmental disability from her previous marriage. After our sons Conor and Cormac were born, we had to seek residential care for Nina. And when we ran out of money, we had to move Nina to an institution known as Willowbrook State School.

When we began poking around Willowbrook we discovered large wards filled with people of all ages screaming, blubbering, some completely naked in pools of their own excrement. Some of them sat banging their heads against the wall, causing their blood to flow and mix with the stinking mess on the floor. For fun, some of the attendants had the beleaguered inmates put on sex shows for them. It was a deplorable warehouse of humanity; a notorious place where the most vulnerable human beings were horribly neglected and abused.

Diana and I, along with the relatives of some of the inmates, formed a liaison with radical staff members and a young attorney and television reporter named Geraldo Rivera to expose the innermost savagery of a shocking and inhuman system. Our daughter Nina joined a list of people led by the ACLU and the Legal Aid Society in a lawsuit that took five years and eventually closed down Willowbrook forever, releasing nearly six thousand citizens into relative freedom in their home communities with appropriate support. Nina went on to live a relatively normal life in an apartment with two roommates and 24-hour care, and beyond Willowbrook, there emerged a legal precedent that has changed the lives of people with developmental difficulties in this country forevermore.

At his inauguration, our first Irish-American president said, "Ask not what your country can do for you, ask what you can do for your country." I came to America thinking only about what it could do for me. But helping to change this system for all of America is one of my proudest achievements.

ACKNOWLEDGMENTS

In addition to the contributors to this anthology, we're grateful to City Winery and its CEO Michael Dorf for hosting another Read650 live event on stage at The Loft. Thanks, too, for the production support of City Winery's Paul Bacher, Marc Coletti, and Jenny Palumbo. **CityWinery.com**

Our thanks to nonprofits consultant and strategist Susan Ragusa, whose free monthly Nonprofits TALK strengthens the nonprofit community in New York's Hudson River Valley through monthly workshop/trainings that address common organizational challenges (thanks, also, to Nonprofits TALK attendees David Congdon and Stephen Wilder of Flying Cat Music for connecting Read650 with Carnegie Hall). **SusanJRagusa.com**

Special thanks to Adriaan Fuchs of Carnegie Hall for including Read650 in its *Migrations: The Making of America* festival. We're very proud to align our name with yours. **CarnegieHall.org**

Nancy Manocherian's *the cell* supported Read650 at its inception. A twenty-first century salon in the heart of New York City, their mission is to support the arts and to incubate new works, and *the cell* made its beautiful performance space available to Read650 as we were finding our way. The cell: To mine the mind, pierce the heart, and awaken the soul. **TheCellTheatre.org**

Artists Without Walls was created to inspire, uplift and unite people and communities of diverse cultures through the pursuit of artistic achievement, and has supported and encouraged Read650 from its beginnings. No Limits. No Walls. No Boundaries. **ArtistsWithoutWalls.com**

READ650.COM

INFO @READ650.COM
FACEBOOK.COM/READ650

www.ingramcontent.com/pod-product-compliance
Lightning Source LLC
Chambersburg PA
CBHW072044170626
46811CB00008B/3154